The Art of Influencing People

A Guide to Effective Communication - How to Read People, Understand their Psychological Needs & Make them Follow Along by Leveraging on Body Language & Public Speaking

George Green

Copyright © [2021] [George Green]

All rights reserved.

The author of this book owns the exclusive right to its content. Any commercial usage or reproduction requires the clear consent of the author.

ISBN: 9798713346232

Table of Contents

Chapter 1 Only 5% of Humans Know the Truth About Successful Influencing 1

    All Influencers Create Value 4

    Share Knowledge, Answer Tough Questions, and Draw Feedback 6

    10 Unmistakable Traits of the Best Influencers 7

Chapter 2 Effective Communication and Influencing: Two Sides of a Coin 12

    Public Speaking vs Negotiation 15

    A One-Size-Fits-All Style to Influencing? 17

    Influencing is a Tactical Game 18

Chapter 3 Influencing Technique 1 – Audience Control 19

    The subtle ability to engage the crowd 21

Chapter 4 Influencing Technique 2 – Putting Yourself in the Shoes of Others 27

    What you want to say vs what the audience wants to hear 30

Chapter 5 Influencing Technique 3 – Read Minds and Expectations 33

What's the fuss about reading minds and expectations, by the way? 35

How do you read the minds of others? 36

Leverage Your Audience's Psychological Needs 38

Chapter 6 Influencing Technique 4 – Channeling Single Narratives 40

Make your audience change their perceptions joyfully 47

Chapter 7 Influencing Technique 5 – Make Yourself Famous 48

Create a Personal Style and Be Noticeable 53

Chapter 8 Influencing Technique 6 – Hard Truth: You Can't Influence Everyone 55

Know Who's Flexible and Who Will Bite Back 59

Chapter 9 Influencing Technique 7 – Influence with More than Words 63

Go above and beyond to Make the World Learn from You 66

Chapter 10 Influencing Technique 8 – Win All Your Arguments Except... 70

Concede a little to appear human 77

Chapter 11 Influencing Technique 9 – Develop Trust and Commitment 79

    Recognize yourself as an infallible authority and stay true 83

Chapter 12 Influencing Technique 10 – Starve Distractions, Feed Appropriate Body Language 87

    Look, Touch, and Move like a God 92

Chapter 13 Plan a Thousand Times over 95

    Effective Communication as a Battle of Ideologies 99

    Plan the How and What beforehand 100

Disclaimer 102

Chapter 1
Only 5% of Humans Know the Truth About Successful Influencing

*The Influential man is the Successful man,
whether he be rich or poor*
~ Orison Swett Marden

Did the opening quote make you feel uneasy? I can bet it did. No one wants to be poor but the overarching mistake 95% of the world makes is to think influence is a by-product of riches. While riches translate to popularity, riches will never give you influence. And if influence is what you crave, regardless of your financial status, then you must learn hidden secrets of how to seize this ability. Within the pages of this book lie those secrets – known by only 5% of the 7 billion people in the world. And there's no better way to start opening this bank of tricks than by reeling out the life of one of the world's most influential persons.

History isn't a popular subject these days. But sometime back in 1980, America witnessed a landmark election that didn't only change the course of history but also provided lessons for as many as could see it. Ronald Reagan, who had recently quit a successful acting career to become governor, picked up the Republican presidential nomination form. He would later win the Presidential election by a LANDSLIDE (The word "landslide" is overused this day, but for context, Ronald Reagan had 90.89% of the electoral college votes in that election).

At the time he won this election, he was 69 years old, making him the oldest elected president at that period. He was conservative in a period when liberalism was thriving in American society. He was an A-list actor in a period where America needed a charismatic Cold War leader.

What's more?

Ronald Reagan was going against the incumbent president of the United States!

Now, while 95% of the world saw a victory that changed America's political climate, the rare 5% of observers saw the virtue of all virtues –INFLUENCE. To be sure, personal influence won the 1980 US Presidential election and not political ideology or favoritism.

Not surprisingly, the good old president was referred to as "The Great Communicator" because he could divide into the thoughts of millions of Americans and bring them along into his mindset. How then does this help you? Reagan was an embodiment of exemplary qualities only 5% of the world has been able to either understand or replicate.

What then is this truth about being influential that only a small fraction of the people you see daily realize? Well, it simply is that influential people are intentional people!

People who wield influence do not just speak, think, or act. They ALWAYS have a goal or purpose in mind. Just like Ronald Reagan, the day-to-day choices of influential people are the result of a mindset that wants to achieve a central goal. All other pleasures will have to give way for their all-embracing life objective.

If you'd ever influence people at any time in your life, you must exude intentionality.

All Influencers Create Value

Point me to an influencer that does not create value, and I'll pay you a billion dollars!

You may be willing to ask if social media influencers fall within this context. I'll counter-ask; why shouldn't they? The creation of value cuts across every niche of influencing – social media, politics, leadership, lifestyle, entertainment, or sports.

No one gains a large, cult-like following without possessing the power of influence. Every influencer can see through each of your psychological needs and present you with a cure to your craving. That is what influencers do. The cure to your craving is the value they offer. And in turn, you constantly look to them to feed upon and nurse your every desire. That's the inextricable link every human being shares with a person who has influence over them.

The average scientist craves global recognition for his work and an authoritative label for his research. So, they hope to be like Thomas Edison or Albert Einstein. They read their books, study their lifestyles, and follow their research pattern. 95% of you see a scientist who aims to succeed. 5% of the world sees a scientist who is under the influence of greater humans who have at different times in history created value.

The same goes for videos, pictures, songs, books, and illustrations that feed your desires, good and bad. The single moment you find a personality that whets your appetite (creates value that you enjoy), you necessarily fall under their influence. And that is the way of the world. You don't influence before you create value. You influence because you already create value.

As you now know, value is relative; the value can be good or bad. In fact, what represents value to someone else may be utter foolishness to you. So, the value you create considers the people for whom you create it. Are you getting set on your journey to being an influential personality? Be set to create value that the people around you recognize as value. Only then can you be an influence.

Share Knowledge, Answer Tough Questions, and Draw Feedback

Only 5% of the world admit that influence is hard work. It involves being intentional about every step you take in life. It revolves around the value you create, which most often than not consumes time and effort. Also, influence is centered on usefulness. Usefulness, in itself, involves building yourself to carry substance that others can share in.

Everyone wants to feel relevant. Also, that is your biggest key to influence. For most people, their relevance comes with how much they know. So, be ready to pump them with relevant knowledge. Show them your wealth of knowledge, and you'll immediately gain their respect.

With statements of knowledge come tough questions that you must be ready to provide answers to. So, being a positive influence involves wide experience and knowledge of how the world works. In fact, more importantly, is how well you can anticipate tough questions from the people you influence. Then, you prepare ahead and let off an aura of confidence and invincibility.

A small fraction of the world's population understands that feedback is integral to their lives as influencers. That's why they constantly push for it. Influencers engage people through whatever means of communication they choose. If you are making a bold step to leave your comfort zone and create the image of an influencer, you must be ready to naturally attract feedback.

10 Unmistakable Traits of the Best Influencers

How do you recognize an influencer? That's a tough query, especially as you must have the lives of hundreds of personalities flashing through your mind as you look for what they all have in common. Save yourself the stress. Here are 10 unmistakable traits every influencer must possess.

Influencers have an eye for the future

Ordinary people fear what will befall them in a post-pandemic world. Influencers look to shape the outcomes of a post-pandemic world. A case in point is Elon Musk, arguably one of the 21st Century's greatest influencers (We probably don't get to see much around anymore). While the rest of the world worried about what to make out of a pandemic-stricken planet, Elon was set to channel the world to Mars. Now, that's some futuristic thinking you should buy into.

Influencers are fearless

Influencers speak and act without fear. They are intentional, so they do not fidget over outcomes. They have thought up multiple options and results, and nothing gets them by surprise. You can only imagine the sort of confidence that flows from such a mind.

Influencers are patient

Absolutely no one grew into a large-scale influencer overnight. Your favorite influencers knew well to build from scratch and nurture their dreams with patience till they blossomed.

Influencers are big on experiments

The influencer is the risk-taker, willing to subject every next best thing to the test. That doesn't mean influencers are mindless or given to impulses. Instead, they see potential and invest heavily in it.

Influencers are relatable

If influencers weren't everyday people, you'd block them out of your life the first minute you meet. On the flip side, influencers know human struggles and reveal them.

Influencers are creative

Creativity is a given for anyone who is on track to being an influence. The restricted view on creativity (acting, singing, visual arts) is dangerous, though.

Every single individual holds a factory of creative juices within them.

Influencers hold unshakable main values

Influencers change their minds but never their values. Their values are the primary source of influence, so they guard it with utmost jealousy.

Influencers are thoroughly consistent

Many individuals interpret this as meaning influencers hardly make mistakes or rarely change their minds. But that's just as far from the truth as it gets. Influencers are consistent with their ideologies, their characteristics, and niches. Overall, they are consistent with their drive and push for success.

Influencers know how to handle criticisms

The influencer's life is not a rosy one. The good news is that they are the best at concealing the negativity that clouds them. Harsh criticisms, death threats, gossip, and cyberbullying are many forms of negative feedback influencers handle with enviable dexterity.

Influencers have a sense of humor

You don't necessarily have to be Kevin Hart to be an influencer – you could be, though. But you need a sense of humor that can sense tension and infuse laughter. Nothing endears the hearts of men like a good smile that takes away boredom.

Chapter 2
Effective Communication and Influencing: Two Sides of a Coin

I motivate players through communication, being honest with them, having them respect and appreciate your ability and your help
~ Tommy Lasorda

If there is any takeaway, you must understand that effective communication and influencing are six and half a dozen. Look at all the traits of an influencer once again. One thing is clear: the best way to see and understand those traits is through effective communication. Never has there been an influencer who could not successfully get across to his audience.

The façade most individuals live under is trying to streamline influencing to a single form of communication. Speaking. Speaking is not the only form of communication influencers can adopt to push boundaries and move mountains. Without different forms of communication, there won't be any type of influence going on around the world.

Effective communication can be a quite cryptic term. Not too many people understand what it means. Therefore, the pages of this chapter will let you in on the true meaning of effective communication and the forms in which it takes.

From fifth grade, you are already aware that communication involves two or more people. As a necessary rule of logic, the effectiveness of such communication is evident when all the parties involved in the exchange leave knowing that their aims have been fulfilled, their needs met, and their intentions understood.

Effective communication is a successful multi-way interaction, nothing more or less.

The key to influencing is effective communication. But the key to effective communication isn't a stroll in the park that we can exhaust in one sentence. It takes a whole lot more.

You can only achieve effective communication when you are aware of your audience's preferred mode of communication and you deliver on it excellently. So, in a class of students with hearing impairments, you will never achieve effective communication with Toastmasters oratory or Presidential debate rhetoric. A written statement or sign language will go farther and prove better than the most carefully conjured speech.

Effective communication may be verbal or non-verbal. However, as the attention span of people continues to drop, verbal communication will demand more than it ever has since the history of the world. Despite this drop in attention span, two verbal communication techniques still offer unbeatable results in how much they shape influence and enhance communication. They are the twin golden nuggets of public speaking and negotiation.

Public Speaking vs Negotiation

Barack Obama was the indisputable champion of 21st Century oratory during the heydays of his electoral campaign. Several of his speeches sit high up with historical orations like the Gettysburg address and "I Have a Dream". Ask the average American, and they can readily quote along: "There's not a liberal America and a conservative America; there's the United States of America."

These accolades do not go for nothing. They prove how gargantuan Obama's public speaking ability was. Then there's this sad twist to the story. Obama wasn't the best of negotiators. He mostly needed a team to negotiate even the most insignificant of deals. And when he attempted to go all out into negotiating by himself, it attracted woeful results.

So, you see, public speaking does not always translate to negotiation skills and vice versa. Fortunately, you can influence people with either of these abilities. But have you stopped to think how massive your range will be if you attempted to wield both qualities? Limitless is the word.

Public speaking is a more general form of communication. It involves your ability to convince many individuals. A public speaker aims to drive people to action and share knowledge on a subject matter. Negotiation is more streamlined. It is a simple tale of how well you do in making other people see your viewpoint and concede to favorable agreements. Both actions are not one and the same.

The media is replete with how to be a good public speaker, how to plan, calm your nerves, and speak sophisticated grammar. The irony is that none of that gibberish will make you a public speaker. The same applies to negotiations. Firmness and charisma will achieve quite a little. The key to achieving both effectively is using the right words!

Public speakers and negotiators painstakingly choose their words. They understand intentionality and give careful thought to every word they say. Take, for instance, a random person walks up to you and says, "give me your apples, and I'll make you happy" Almost immediately, another random person walks up and says, "your apples are the choicest in America.

I'm willing to offer you fulfilment for every single one of them".

Who are you more poised to surrender your apple to? The one whose words appeal to you the more.

A One-Size-Fits-All Style to Influencing?

Go into a room full of diverse people and say the word "influence". People will conjure up different names. And when you look closely, everyone has built within their mind a stereotype of what influence means. To some, influence is all about leadership; to others, they interpret it as entertainment, or a Forbes recognized level of wealth. These are too many convenient stereotypes we force ourselves into.

Grasping the art of influence will require you to shed those stereotypes and embrace the bigger picture. There is no one-size-fits-all style to influencing. Think about it, Walt Disney influences with cartoons. There is a tool in your hand that is a potential weapon of influence. Will you wait till it translates into the idea of influence you have conjured for yourself? Or will you chart a course of influence with whatever creative ability you see within you?

Influencing is a Tactical Game

Promising yourself to lead a life of influence is a bold step, but do you realize what you are setting yourself up for? Being an influence carries the responsibility to adopt warlike tactics. It is you versus the thoughts and deep-seated opinions of tens, thousands, and millions of others. You need more than words of affirmation and determination. You need a proven strategy that can convert you from an individual battling for recognition to a being that commands reverence.

The ten techniques to carving influence are what you need. And it starts right on the turning of the page.

Chapter 3
Influencing Technique 1 – Audience Control

*A good teacher, like a good entertainer,
first must hold his audience's attention,
then he can teach his lesson.
~ John Henrik Clarke*

A young chap once told me that if Mathematics was reduced to memes, he still wouldn't find the subject a tad interesting. And many of us can share a similar sentiment with different subjects we came across at high school or in college. We realized how extremely taxing it was to maintain flair for several academic courses we found uninteresting. The sad part is that our teachers had to bear the brunt of the reaction from students who could not stay on course because they disliked a subject. Now, that ought to give an insight into what happens when an audience is uninterested in an activity.

The big question is if you were made to handle an audience who had no flair for a subject matter, would you get the most of their concentration and interest?

If you are unsure of your answer, there is a 99% chance you will fare poorly. The good news is that you don't have to. Engaging people – bored, tired, and worn-out people – doesn't have to be as hard as time travel. With the singular key of audience control, you can wake a slumbering crowd and draw them to you.

Influencing, in any form, is purely the act of telling people where to find a treasure without visibly showing them. So, there is an abundance of gold out there, and you want your audience to go for it. You can't make them see the gold physically. You can't even bring them to touch it. Nonetheless, you want them to pursue it. You want it to be theirs. To achieve this lofty goal, you need to make your audience believe you first. You need to assert authority and show them all that you've been there. You have felt the gold. You've, in fact, taken some for yourself, and now it is their time to get theirs.

This singular action is audience control. And while it is a major key to capturing attention in public speaking, it works outside of it. Controlling your audience is simply gaining command over them, bringing their short attention spans into submission. No audience is ready to stay with you long. Humans can't maintain maximum concentration for more than 8 seconds… that is about the average attention span. Yet you want to keep people glued to you for four minutes, a quarter of an hour, an hour, half a day, or even weeks. You won't achieve this if you can't control your crowd.

The subtle ability to engage the crowd

Does control sound like a strong word? It sure does. But nothing comes close to describing the effect you must make on the people you seek to influence than control. With all that has been said and done, how do you achieve this control?

The only way to get your audience on your side is to engage them. Remember the opening quote? You must first hold your audience's attention before you teach your lesson. Or else, every word, every action will fall on deaf ears and barren minds.

Engaging the crowd is a form of entertainment. It circles around making them interested in whatever you are about to say or do. There must be a strong force that holds them down so much they aren't willing to leave you until you give all that is there to offer.

The greatest influencers of all time have employed several techniques to engage their audience and leave them captivated. I have summed up every of their audience control strategy to three. As a professional advice piece, the more of these strategies you can lay hold on, the better for you and your audience. So, why not dig in and find which strategies are perfectly fitting your personality and line of influence.

Put your features to good use

Many a time, we hear the rather hackneyed advice: use what you have to get what you need. That is no less true in influencing any group of people. There are physical features every audience is triggered by. The most common is beauty. Human beings are made to appreciate beauty. That's why we are tourists. That's why we have beauty pageants. If you are high on the beauty side, it is a potent weapon in your arsenal. Exploit it to the maximum, whether you be male, female, or even if you are a clown in a costume.

The next feature you must put to good use is your voice charm. You have scintillating vocal cords? Then you've hit the jackpot. You get compliments on how deep your voice cracks? Then you're in big luck. Your opening sentence every time you speak should send everyone asking for more.

Whatever your key feature is, make it a point of call to exploit it in a way that leaves your audience in awe. And if nature did not bestow you with any, remember that Marilyn Monroe was once a stutterer. Make what you will with that information.

Killer introductions

You probably saw this coming. But what is any form of communication without a killer introduction? Introductions are the pathway into the life you hope to offer your audience. They see a glimpse of the value you are up to offer, and they are eager to consume the total package.

Introductions are most important when you aim to influence your audience through public speaking. One primary method that many speakers have exploited over the years is the power of storytelling introductions.

In 1948, immediately after the Cold War, a Jewish couple forced to travel to the US from Germany, started a coffee shop…

If you were eager to hear a story, I'm sorry to disappoint but there is none. Regardless, it is certain that you must have anticipated the next paragraph, hoping to know more about a fictional tale or a real-life event. If you can feel the impact of a good story before it even starts, your audience will feel no different.

Still on killer introductions, you must not underestimate the power of questions. A thoughtful, comical, or knowledge-based (did you know) question can do the trick perfectly. Most often than not, killer introductions will give you a pedestal to start your influence on. What you then make of it is entirely up to you.

Be Interactive

Has a test ever been your sole motivation for paying attention in class? Or have you ever watched a YouTube video until the end based on the promise of secret information or a giveaway at the end of the show? That is exactly how being interactive works. You work to engage your audience by making them feel like a part of the entire process.

If you intend to exercise a great deal of influence over your audience, you must rein them in while still maintaining your control. The promise of a gift, secret information, a quiz, and so on can make your audience pay attention and interact better with all you have in store.

Chapter 4
Influencing Technique 2 – Putting Yourself in the Shoes of Others

To be a good citizen, it is important to be able to put yourself in other people's shoes and see the big picture. If everything you see is rooted in your own identity, that becomes difficult or impossible.
~ Eli Pariser

The truth is being a good citizen is not the only motivation you'll need to put yourself in other people's shoes. If you are on the path to influencing, you will find that this tip comes in handy too. And I'm going to dive right deep into what it means to put yourself into the shoes of others. As you must already know, the phrase has nothing to do with Louboutin or

Nike footwear. But it has got everything to do with empathy and mutual understanding.

Influencing is a game of numbers. Numbers, in their plural form. You start to consider yourself an influencer when you can consciously name two disciples who see you as a source of inspiration. Take a moment to consider the world's greatest footballers in this age: Cristiano Ronaldo and Lionel Messi. They are literally revered by millions of people, even though only a very tiny fraction of the people who consider them as influences play professional football. How do these stars achieve this level of influence?

Quite simple. They put themselves in the shoes of the millions of people who come to watch them live and on TV.

Every football fan screams for a win, goals, dribbles, and interesting football. These stars understand this feeling far too well. They've been spectators themselves before they became stars, so they know what the average fan expects. This way, it becomes easy for them to deliver and gain the crowd's confidence. They put themselves in your shoes as a spectator. They ask themselves what you would expect from them, and they go all out to put up a fine display. That's simple logic and arithmetic.

However, it can get tougher in some areas. I can easily tell the reason you are on this page is that you want to learn empathy. This knowledge makes me one step ahead in shaping every word in this chapter. But I can't say the same when I walk into a conference room filled with Fortune 500 chief executives, entrepreneurs, and Silicon Valley leaders. They all have different perceptions of business, profit, technology, and leadership. How do I put myself in the shoes of people with diverse backgrounds and attitudes?

The answer is not too far off. There is a common shoe we all wear. There is a common denominator in every human gathering, an ideology that levels every individual within that space and time. At a protest ground, it is the sense of justice and fairness. At a business gathering, it is the desire for a feasible, profitable, and sustainable business model. At a religious gathering, it is faith. Regardless of prior intention, the common denominator makes it easy for everyone to agree on several basics. The common denominator is your key to influence any group of individuals on the earth's surface.

At every given time in your life, find the common denominator amidst a group of people and exploit it like you've only got one chance at it. Well, maybe because you really do. But you shouldn't miss the point.

If you must achieve the goal of influencing, your first entry into a room full of people should not be marred by pleasantries. Consider the different factions in the room. What brings them together? What have they been through? What are their expectations? Once you find answers, leave room for no further questions.

What you want to say vs what the audience wants to hear

It would be unrealistic to pretend that there are no times when ideologies clash and you do not believe in a jot of what the people you seek to influence believe in. Surely, there are times when the common denominator is a concept you hate with all your innermost.

If you are caught in this web, you have two options. You can either say and do what's on your mind and lose your audience irredeemably. On the other hand, you can do what a maestro will do.

What will a maestro do?

Good question. A maestro will find the balance. Influencing is people centered. You revolve around your audience, so your audience can revolve around you. That is the process influencing follows, and this doesn't bend for anyone.

Finding the balance involves you making your audience know that two truths can coexist. Imagine you were made to convince people that trees grow on rocks, even though they believed something entirely different (you know this by being in their shoes). Your job is to make them realize that all rocks are not the same! Soil debris in some rocks can make trees grow, while other rocks can kill the seeds. Then you leave them to try it out. Whatever outcome they get, it is a win-win for you. You did not mislead them, yet you did not go back on what you aimed to say.

You must be ready to strike a balance between what the audience wants to hear and what you intend to say.

There is a caveat, though. Going back on life truths is not worth the blind loyalty of a couple of followers. There is a greater common denominator you must never sacrifice – humanity!

Chapter 5
Influencing Technique 3 – Read Minds and Expectations

It's easy to read someone's mind
when you understand their feelings
~ Dilwaalikudi

You may come to wonder how whether reading minds and putting yourself in other shoes aren't substantially different. You have valid queries. But for all intents and purposes, as far as influencing humans is concerned, they are two distinct principles.

Putting yourself in another's shoes is primarily the act of trying to understand the backgrounds of your audience and their motivations. Putting yourself in another's shoes is an act that helps you evaluate how the past affects the present.

On the other hand, reading minds and expectations is an action in the present. The mind is in a continuous free flow. It thinks and expects in the present. While personal backgrounds and other factors may affect it, the mind mainly works independently of these factors in several cases.

Also, the previous chapter urged you to understand the common denominators in your audience before you start a showdown. Reading minds is an entirely different ball game. It calls for an ongoing process of projecting and reaching into the innermost thoughts of your audience. At different intervals, you need to be able to read the minds, emotions, and thoughts of your audience.

Now that you already realize the difference between reading minds and empathy, we might as well dive properly into why and how this process must take place.

What's the fuss about reading minds and expectations, by the way?

There's a big fuss. And it is justified. You have every reason to want to read the minds of the people you influence. Unlike programmed machines and robots, human thoughts and emotions are very flexible. One minute they are in love, and the next minute, they can swear they disgust your every being.

So, you must be fully on the ground to read and process this changing thought pattern.

Moreover, reading minds and expectations help you finetune your thoughts and actions. Your ability to tell what your followers are thinking at a particular point allows you to play the music they love to listen to. The ability to read minds impacts the power and force of your communication like no other. You suddenly find yourself saying the right words and doing agreeable deeds.

Reading minds is both a superpower and a teachable process. But you must distinguish what's telepathy from psychology. Telepathy is a farce created by media. However, psychology is real life. It's a tangible ability we see in everyday humans like you and me.

Just like psychologists, the power to read minds or at least tell the emotional patterns of an individual will come in handy if your aim is to influence, heal, or convince people.

How do you read the minds of others?

Reading minds and predicting expectations doesn't come easy. You're the leader of a group of people, and you want to keep in step with their needs without asking them. Believe me, that is a very honorable yet lofty goal. But it's not impossible.

You simply require the power of perception and emotional intelligence to successfully read the minds of any member of an audience. Almost every human being communicates their thoughts at different intervals. It's up to you to pick up their flashing signals and predict what's rocking their minds or the expectations they create in their inner chambers.

Here are several ways to read minds and predict expectations successfully.

Locate the emotional triggers

You can tell what a person is thinking by their reaction to situations, their words, and actions. To get their emotions out, you must say and do the things that elicit a response. Whatever response you get from them will determine whether they are happy, sad, or plainly apathetic to you.

This strategy is one you must adopt at every point of your influence. Otherwise, you will lose your followers midway without even realizing it.

Patience

This tip sure looks like a dog that has lost its way to a cat race. Yet, in all sincerity, no virtue helps you read minds as patience does. Those occasional pauses you take during your speech, those moments of inactivity, achieve one integral aim – they reveal the impatience of others. If the ongoing emotion you intend to read is concentration, patience achieves that excellently.

Interact

Interaction is central to the mind-reading process, especially if you want your subject to express their feelings through word cues. Ask the right questions, be attentive and responsive to signals. A good mind reader ensures to go as deeply as possible while engaging the subject in discourse.

Leverage Your Audience's Psychological Needs

Reading minds and predicting expectations is a rather broad concept. And one principal aspect of it that influencers must understand is the aspect of the psychological need.

The first question that arises is, why do you want to read minds? If your response is that so you can know what your audience is thinking, you're not intentional about the process. Rather, your response should be so that you can channel your influence to meet the psychological needs of your followers.

Every attempt at reading minds reveals the emotions, thoughts, and expectations of your audience. In turn, these emotions translate to psychological needs. For instance, an emotion that expresses glee and positivity is a desire for more of what you offer. So, why not continue with your tempo? That way, you would be on a communication level that corresponds with your audience.

Not all human beings will show the same emotions when you probe into their hearts, especially when you run a crowd. That is why it is essential to find common ground throughout the process of mind reading. It gives you an aggregate of the majority of your audience and an avenue to build on your future words and actions.

Chapter 6
Influencing Technique 4 – Channeling Single Narratives

Stories constitute the single most powerful weapon in a leader's arsenal.
~ Howard Gardner

Channeling single narratives is one key step to becoming an influencer. However, it isn't as crystal clear as all other techniques you require as an influencer. Unlike several other tips that you have a fair idea of before picking up this book, this advice is fairly new. Not new in the sense of a 21st-century discovery – the world has seen great influencers since thousands of centuries BC. But it is new in the sense of it being a hidden tool in the hands of a select few.

In this chapter, we will differentiate channeling single narratives from different concepts that look like it, including those that have been discussed in previous chapters.

As a starting point, there's the need to show you that channeling single narratives is entirely different from telling people what they want to hear. In the latter situation, you are about to strike a balance between several contradictory thoughts and opinions. However, with single narratives, you are giving a full and final version of how a story should go. And get it clear, it is not the use of force or some sort of dogmatism – quite the opposite. Channeling single narratives involves being able to convince people to stick to one truth. So, you may consider it an advanced form of finding a balance between contradictory ideas.

If an example will help, here's one. Assume you are in a lecture room with scholars, and they now consider you as a primary influence in their careers. If there are divergent views on your personality, would you rather seek to strike a balance or create a single narrative about yourself? As sure as eggs are eggs, you would want to give them a single, comprehensive version of what and who you are. That is what channeling single narratives revolve around. You'll get to a point in your status as an influencer, and all you must do then is give an authoritative narrative on an idea or person – no highway options.

Moving forward, there's a big difference between channeling single narratives and building stereotypes. These concepts are two parallel lines that will never meet, not in this life, nor in the next. Stereotypes are hyper-generalized opinions about people. In channeling single narratives, your task is to make people understand and be convinced that there is only one narrative to this concept or idea. You make statements of facts and not of opinion. Stereotypes, on the other hand, are unfounded statements of opinion.

The overarching question you may want to ask is, why should you even bother about channeling single narratives? Well, you should bother about channeling single narratives because they tell your story. They say all about you and what you represent.

During the American Civil War, the great debate among scholars, politicians, scientists, and influencers of every sort was whether slavery was unjust or justifiable. This singular notion will divide America for decades, with fragments still palpable to this day.

During this period of scholastic back and forth, a particular individual who channeled a single narrative came forward. That single narrative has, over the years, transformed to cement his name as one of the greatest leaders in history. That's not all. His singular narrative has grown to be the foundation upon which modern American politics and liberal ideology is founded. The man was Abraham Lincoln.

In the heat of the Civil War, Abraham Lincoln was frequently asked about his opinions on slavery. Mind you, this question goes down to the root of his rise to influence. The American society wanted a single story they could adopt as their central ideology, an objective viewpoint that will explain all that is to live in the new America they clamored for. Not too many people were willing to deliver on this deal till Abraham Lincoln took a leap forward. Lincoln had not always been against slavery, but the moment he built up the totality of his beliefs, he was more than willing to have the world know about them. He was ready to shout his ideals from the rooftops.

That process isn't exclusive to Abraham Lincoln. Every influencer has at one point in history or the other, channeled the single narratives they intend to stand by throughout their careers. That is because such narratives and viewpoints are integral to their influence. Such viewpoints are their personal stories, legacies that will outlive them. So, on your journey to influence, consider first the single narrative you will want the world to consider as your signature story.

These narratives are also the key to building your follower base. No one wants to make a model out of an influencer who isn't ready to take a stand with courage and tell their story. In fact, single narratives transcend important matters like slavery, racism, terrorism, or other deep global issues. In whatever area of life you intend to be an influence, you cannot choose to be a prostitute of ideas. Remember that influencers change their minds and not their values or central idea.

As an actor, a sportsperson, an author, an entrepreneur, or whatever path life sets you on, always channel a single story that speaks volumes about you.

As much as possible, you should also give careful thought to your single narratives. You do not want to follow a pattern or central idea that will come back to sting you.

In a world where people are too pliable and indifferent to the notions that shape society, be an influence by channeling single narratives. And what is a single narrative without people who are convinced by it?

That leads to the next critical issue. Convince people about your objective truth. I know this sounds like a struggle, but this is the foundation on which your influence either falls or stands. How do you make this work?

Courage and Conviction

You can't convince other people if you aren't convinced yourself. It will take a great, visible deal of conviction on your part to channel your single narrative.

Be logical yet flattery

Always be sure to make the most sense in your arguments for what you stand by. A foolish thought is not worth conjuring; talk less of defending such thought. That's why you must give careful thought to your narratives. And when that is done, present it in a logical flow and be flexible enough to flatter the other party of its benefits to them. Imagine if the abolition of slavery as put out by Abraham Lincoln was a selfish idea. You can almost see the death of such a narrative before it even got to the public scene.

Be persistent yet patient

No one will take in your single narrative at a full gulp. You need to apply pressure, back off a little, apply pressure, back off a little, and repeat the cycle till you achieve your goals.

Make your audience change their perceptions joyfully

The greatest form of channeling a single narrative is doing it in such a way that your narrative can make your audience change their opinions without breaking a sweat. What other people achieve with fallible hypnosis; you must be ready to achieve with the right tools.

Every opportunity to channel a single narrative is an opportunity to make the rest of the world automatically see things from your perspective. How do you do that?

Your story should involve you speaking with your audience, not speaking at them. Engage them in the process of channeling the narrative. Use logic and flattery to get the task done efficiently.

Chapter 7
Influencing Technique 5 –
Make Yourself Famous

Define what your brand stands for,
its core values and tone of voice,
and then communicate consistently in those terms.
~ Simon Mainwaring

Every year, about 15,000 lives are saved because of the revolutionary invention of one man, done as far back as 1959.The brain behind such groundbreaking work must be so famous, you would think. Sadly, he isn't. Hardly is his activity recognized in contemporary books or school curriculum. His act remains one of the most influential deeds on the planet. But quite unfortunately, his personality does not qualify as much to be regarded as an influence.

This sad story is the life reality of Nils Bohlin. Nils Bohlin is the engineer who invented the seat belt while he worked for Volvo. Over 60 years after this amazing invention, tens of thousands of people preserve their lives merely by putting the seat belt on. If you ask me, Nils Bohlin should rank as highly as Alexander Fleming, Henry Ford. Karl Benz, Alexander Graham Bell and the biggest inventors of the 19th and 20th Century. Yet, he doesn't. Not because he didn't meet the criteria to be such a great influence but because he failed to make himself famous.

At the beginning of this book, I clarified two major principles. The first was that influencers aren't necessarily wealthy. And that's a given. A popular case in point was Mahatma Gandhi, the Indian ruler who came from a poor background and remained just slightly above the lower class during his lifetime. But the interesting part of Gandhi's life was that his $1000 net worth did not deter him from being a great influence on colonialism and politics in India and globally.

The second principle at the start of this book was that influencers create value. Every example that this book has examined were people who had sufficient value to dole out to people, regardless of their age, orientation, or status.

Nils Bohlin met all these requirements, yet he didn't rise to the status of an influencer because he failed to make himself famous. Making yourself famous is at the heart of being a success at everything you do. Unlike what is the general opinion, making yourself famous as an influencer does not stem from pride or vainglory. Instead, it's a necessary tool you require if you must scale the value of your offer and gain the recognition you deserve.

If you have wise words to say and you're confined to your bedroom, no one will hear it save your roommates. If you're lucky enough, the birds by your window will project your ideas. But you will never get the fitting audience to listen to you. The same goes for every activity in life: sports, fashion, entertainment, business, politics. You need to positively send yourself into the spotlight to even be regarded as an influencer to start with. Every influencer you know has that name tag because they were not confined to their immediate environment.

What's the charge for you?

Break free and break forth. Let the value you possess be known across the four cardinal points of the planet.

As you must have noticed throughout this book, there's no good in telling people what to do if you're not going to show them. This chapter will show you all you need to tap into the greatness that lies ahead of you.

How then can you be famous?

Stand by a Cause

Much has been said about channeling a single narrative, but this chapter requires another emphasis. You can build a name for yourself by choosing a valuable cause and standing by it. A "cause" does not necessarily translate to a philanthropic ideal or a trending global issue. It could be your flair or a means of entertainment you connect to. Your "cause" must be a phenomenon you have a natural affiliation to. And when you find it, cling to it, and remain consistent with actions that strengthen your affiliation to such an idea.

Build Relationships

It is popularly said that your network is your net worth. However, such statements tend to create an underlying perception of your relationships as translating to commercial value. Relationships should be mutually beneficial and geared towards helping all parties involve leverage skill sets and potential value. For the purpose of pushing your influence, build vertical and horizontal relationships with people who can push your value to the world.

Use Social Media

The world has gone past the days when influence was defined by how many podiums you've been invited to speak at. The world is now a global village, and the condition of the world doesn't seem like it will be changing in a decade or more. Create social media accounts on several platforms and let the world see the form of value you possess and have to offer.

Create a Personal Style and Be Noticeable

The crux of being an influencer is branding. Asides from being popular, you need to have a brand. You need to have distinct features that set you apart from your contemporaries. You should capitalize on your idiosyncrasies and transform them into an identity. Random people ought to tell your presence by mere fragments of your personality. That is what a personal brand is all about.

Personal branding is just like having a concept or an idea synonymous with you. Just like carbonated drinks are synonymous with Coca-Cola or burgers synonymous with McDonald's, you should have a distinguishing feature that people can readily link to you.

A good example of a personal brand is Elon Musk. The entrepreneur has grown in leaps and bounds to become one of the biggest brands in the world. Any reference to Elon Musk is usually synonymous with space travel, cryptocurrency, and electric cars. At a point, he was even the richest man in the world. So, hardly is there a mention of an enterprising individual without Elon Musk being at the center of the discussion, or at least, having some worthy mention.

You want to build a brand for yourself? Then put out your peculiarities, offline and online. Don't shy away from opportunities that tend to amplify your voice and what you represent. On the contrary, actively seek such platforms.

Also, surround yourself with individuals who will recommend you without thinking twice. You can't get to the top all by yourself, neither can you get to your peak overnight. It starts with a small recommendation to speak at an event, a call to lead an organization, and an intentional post on your social media. In no time, you'll find out that you've set the stage to be a world-class influencer.

Chapter 8
Influencing Technique 6 – Hard Truth: You Can't Influence Everyone

No matter how hard you try,
you can never please everyone.
Follow your heart, make the most of every day,
and be proud of who you are.
~ John Cena

On the road to being a top influencer, you'll always find drawbacks until you realize that you are your own worst enemy.

Now, you may wonder what this opening paragraph has got to do with the headline of the chapter. Well, they have more connections than one, especially if you're looking at the bigger picture.

Let's talk about the people-pleasing disease.

If you're able to read this book at all, chances are that you're old enough and you can relate to the idea behind people-pleasers.

People pleasers are simply individuals who think they can get on the good side of everyone. They make every attempt to get the approval of friends, family members, and even strangers. For people-pleasers, saying "no" is an entirely impossible task. They'll rather stick a baobab tree into their nostrils than get a negative comment about themselves from the fellow next door.

That is disgusting, and everyone knows. But look at the mirror, and you'll see that there's the trait of a people-pleaser in yourself. It's a disease, and it's inherent in every human being. Only that it comes in differing quantities for everyone. While there's the individual down the road who would rather die than not suck up to everyone he meets, there's another fellow who can be firm with everyone else except her children. There's a bit of a people pleaser in everybody.

Your people-pleasing trait may cause you to shy away from speaking out your mind when it's most necessary to the people who need it the most. Besides, you tell yourself that you dread conflicts and the best way to be immune to potential disagreements is to just do ALL that the people around you want. This attitude keeps you from having a mind of your own. You will end up being a shadow of yourself and losing the real you to unworthy circumstances.

How does this affect you as an influencer? I would say influencers are most affected by the people-pleasing disease. I've been there, and I can tell the exact tale of what it means to be bound by this disease while trying to be an influence on people around you.

The sad reality about influencing is that you do not lose your emotions. If you're rash by nature, except you undergo a drastic change, you'll grow into a rash influencer. If you're impulsive, you'd naturally become an influencer who is subject to their whims and caprices rather than logic and experience.

For me, starting out as an influencer meant I had to speak to large groups of people, share my experience as an entrepreneur, channel my single narrative and lead people to see how they can make a profit from businesses. Just about then, I would get calls about how great I was doing on one hand and how some people didn't think I was giving them what they wanted on the other. This sort of feedback made me panic greatly. I was out to please everyone. More than that, I was out to influence everyone! Guess what? It didn't work out. It didn't work out because it can never work out.

You simply CANNOT INFLUENCE EVERYBODY.

If you could influence everybody, the world will have one religion, one political ideology, one system of ethics, one method of making money, and you name them. In fact, there would be no need to write this book because we all would probably be learning under the influence of one great leader.

But this realization isn't just enough; you need to also realize your tendencies to want to get everybody on your side – your people-pleasing disease – and deal with them. Your people-pleasing disease is what translates to a false notion that you can please everyone.

Know Who's Flexible and Who Will Bite Back

The people-pleasing train is fast-moving, packing hundreds of millions, if not billions of people along with it. How then do you get yourself off this train that is heading to career destruction?

First, you need to know the traits of people you can influence and those that are out of your control.

There are three main reasons why someone will be out of your control despite you having all that it takes to be a world-class influence. It may be that the person is an influencer who knows exactly what you know and won't change their values just like you wouldn't change yours. It could also be that such an individual is naturally averse to learning or naturally dogmatic. And finally, that person may merely have extraordinarily strong inclinations to a different ideology or brand. You know what, such situations are entirely fine. But you must be able to recognize them, so you don't risk having your time wasted.

Traits of people you can influence	Traits of people you can't influence
They give you general feedback about your influence	They ask questions to put you down
They put you up to opportunities and larger platforms to showcase yourself	They try to discourage you from taking up bigger projects
You can see bits of your style in them	They tend to talk down on your style and visibly counter it
They learn from you and create something similar	They copy you with the intention to compete with you
They do little things to get your attention (like following you on social media and sending you cold emails)	They have no remembrance of what your ideologies or style looks like. Instead, they challenge and criticize your every move. Most times, they are indifferent to your progress

If you notice the trends, then you'll need to do sifting and sorting of your followership. Channel your energy to people who are more responsive to you and systematically cut off all those who display traits adverse to your influence.

When you realize that not everyone will cheer you on when you speak, not everyone will agree with you when you communicate your ideas, not everyone will subscribe to your entertainment, you're building peace for yourself. In fact, you gain greater satisfaction, and you can be your real self. It becomes much easier to communicate your objectives effectively to your audience.

Before we consider the next technique, you've read in other chapters that you should strike a balance between what you want to say and what the audience wants to hear. That is true. But you may be asking, if everyone can't follow me or get the points I talk about, why suffer finding a balance.

The answer is simple, the mere knowledge that everyone isn't going to follow your lead is not a leeway to stop trying entirely. Having separate ideologies does not always translate to hostility. If you're being honest, you'll discover that most of the people who tend to hold contrary beliefs do so innocently and do not mean to hurt you.

Let the traits table be your guide. Know those you can't influence, but don't let that drag you into acting immaturely or irresponsibly with/to them.

Chapter 9
Influencing Technique 7 – Influence with More than Words

Sometimes our actions are more meaningful than words. A hug can sometimes express more than our words will ever express.
~ Catherine Pulsifer

Influencing and communication are two sides of a coin. But words are sadly overhyped. Now, that may not sit well with many folks who are public speakers. However, I'm not trying to pick a quarrel. I'm not saying words are unimportant; I'm simply saying *words* have been accorded way too much value than they can actually live up to.

Little is said of the great Hellen Keller. Hellen Keller became blind, mute, and deaf at the tender age of 18 months.

Now, take a break from this book and try to communicate to a random person that you're feeling hungry while pretending that you're blind, mute, and deaf.

If my guess is anything to go by, everyone would be stuck. You are unable to write nor read because you can't see, and you're unable to talk nor listen because you can neither speak nor hear. That's the sort of dire situation Hellen Keller was in. If she lived in this era, she could have gotten visual and auditory aids to remedy the deficiencies. Unfortunately, she lived as far back as the late 19th century. There wasn't even a perfect Braille system by them.

Still, Hellen Keller rose to be one of the greatest influencers of ALL time and an effective communicator. She learnt to speak five languages and wrote life-changing books. She did that without saying a word.

What was Hellen Keller's secret?

Hellen Keller discovered that life does not revolve around words but in expression. You may have the ability to speak all the languages in the world, but if you can't find expression for yourself, you can't communicate effectively, neither can you be the great influencer aim to become.

For some people, it will come in words, no doubt. But for others, their mode of expression will be unconventional. If the aim is to communicate and do so effectively, you must find the channel of communication that helps you bring to the fore your deepest thoughts and greatest value.

For many, music is their greatest form of expression. They express their sadness, joy, and indifference better while on a grand piano. You could look at the lives of Beethoven and Mozart for context. These men influenced the world by merely connecting keys on a piano to form a rhythmical pattern. Beethoven may not have as many quotes as Corrie ten Boom or John F. Kennedy, but he influenced the world and communicated as effectively as he could through the instrumentality of music.

Effective communication with the aim of being an influence on other people requires you to make your thoughts and ideas known in the best way possible.

Go above and beyond to Make the World Learn from You

To go above and beyond is to outdo your current limitation, whatever they may be. That journey is multilayered and longer than you have imagined. But you should never walk alone. Hellen Keller had Anne Sullivan teach her the rudiments of communicating and influencing in her state. And in this book, these tips will guide you to find the best way to express yourself, and by extension, influence through effective communication.

Find the mode of communication that gives you the greatest fulfilment

This task may look hard, but with deep introspection, you're good to go. Search introspectively to see what form of communication you do best. If it's speaking, by all means, do not consider it a less glorious or too common medium of expression.

If you're stuck with discovering what mode of communication is your magical wand, you may consider speaking to a friend and letting them guide you through the process of finding expression.

Gain mastery of your communication strength

After discovery, your next point of call is to master your preferred mode of communication. One thing most leaders and life coaches will hide from you is the route to mastery. As much as practice makes perfect, your background development does little if an already existing authority does not confer recognition on you.

Would you visit a doctor without a medical degree? You surely wouldn't because his certificate confers mastery upon him. While you can naturally be an excellent speaker, an expert artist, and so on, you would do yourself much service if you add a formal recognition of your expertise.

So, go to that music school, take up that public speaking course, sign up for that film institute, and watch more people consider you an influence in your chosen field.

Buy favors

If the next idea that pops in your head is giving a bribe, then you're totally far from the truth. Buying favors is not in any way synonymous with bribery. Rather, you can refer to it as the seed and harvest rule. Simply put, you cannot always gain a reputation from people if all you do is talk. You need to back it up with some quality action.

Some of the people you seek to influence will be people in need. You need to be able to reach out to them with utmost care. Meeting the needs of one follower could go a great deal in buying them over to yourself. You never know; your actions could cause a positive chain reaction that may, in fact, change how you influence people.

However, just like with every other tip, learn the boundaries. Afterall, you cannot influence everyone.

Chapter 10
Influencing Technique 8 – Win All Your Arguments Except...

*One of the marks of a truly great mind,
I had discovered, is the ability to feign stupidity
on demand.*
~ Alan Bradley

Do you want to be an effective communicator? Then you must learn the art of feigning ignorance, feigning stupidity, and feigning indifference. A 100% perfect attitude as an influencer could literally cost you your followership.

You need to master the art of intentionally losing some arguments if you must maintain your status as an effective communicator and an influencer. Now, remember, influencing is not a debate where you choose to fight to the finish in a bid to win a prize or gain recognition in the contest. Rather, it's a life-long process of trying to render value to people and gain their followership in their process. If you would be successful at such an intricate human relation as that, you need to be totally relatable.

An individual who constantly tries to force ALL their opinions and tries to always put everyone else in the wrong won't come off as an influencer. Rather, they will be considered a proud, egotistical, and condescending know-it-all. Your aim is to be a positive influence and not earn a bad name in the process, isn't it?

So, there will be a time when the need arises to throw in the towel and let other people get the win. This way, you underline mutual respect and understanding as a core value you possess. Your audience also considers themselves as intelligent people whose opinions matter. That way, you're raking up all the points for yourself as they will consider you more relatable.

Most times, everyone knows where an argument will most likely end. Going back and forth gives them room to manipulate you, force words from your mouth, or even gaslight you in the future. You're placing too much power in the hands of people who should reasonably consider you as a model. That's bad publicity for your status as an influencer.

At other times, some opinions are merely bystander points. If you constantly see the need to reply to every critic and throw stones at every barking dog, you lose valuable time and resources.

As such, it's always important to know the times to stay silent and the moments that you have to go all out.

These situations should, however, not deter your capacity to listen. While not winning arguments, you give yourself every reason to listen and learn from every party involved. With this advantage, you can:

- Increase the value you offer people around you

- Place yourself in other people's shoes

- Easily read the minds of your critics

- Discover those with traits of the people you cannot influence, and

- Influence people with more than just words.

If there's this immense potential that comes with not winning every argument, then it is a technique to apply.

Acts to avoid during disagreements as an influencer and effective communicator

Notably, periods where you have to fake a loss come in moments of disagreement. If you have a common goal, objective or opinion, there will practically be no need for you to fake a loss.

However, in moments of disagreement, many individuals tend to take drastic actions in their frustration. These actions are known to come back to sting the people that took them. Particularly, impatience drives people to argue illogically or engage in a personal attack on their opponent. These are situations you must strive to avoid in your communication as an influencer.

The illustration below says more about specifics you must do away with in any disagreement.

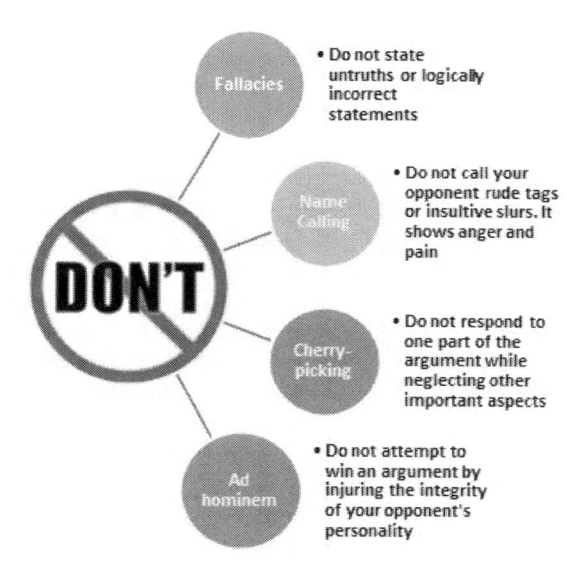

- **Fallacies**: Do not state untruths or logically incorrect statements
- **Name Calling**: Do not call your opponent rude tags or insultive slurs. It shows anger and pain
- **Cherry-picking**: Do not respond to one part of the argument while neglecting other important aspects
- **Ad hominem**: Do not attempt to win an argument by injuring the integrity of your opponent's personality

Measures to take during disagreement as an influencer and effective communicator

On the flip side, when you are set with an unyielding opponent, there are rules of engagement that set an influencer apart from a common debater. The major action you're reasonably expected to take while disagreeing is to argue your points based on verifiable facts. Instead of launching a personal attack on your opponent, puncture his opinions and beliefs with a logically presented line of thought.

Most individuals believe that logic and emotion are the two critical tools of convincing any opponent. Apply these tools. Logic comes with the ability to state facts and apply them to situations. Emotions, however, consists of using soothing language to drive your opinions to your audience.

If you stick to this rule, one thing is certain: You may not be able to get an adamant opponent off the leash, but you'll win followers and influence lots of people who heard you communicate.

The next step is now defining what arguments you must apply the pressures of logic and emotion to as well as the arguments you may reasonably back off from.

How do you identify an argument that you must not win?

It is tough to intentionally give in to an opponent, but some factors should drive you to do this. They include:

Where the opponent has shown signs of not being open to a consensus

If your opponent categorically states that they have no plans to withdraw or even reach a truce on your debate, they are simply showing traits of people that you cannot – and shouldn't bother influencing.

Where the benefits of withdrawing far outweigh the demerits

If you will not suffer a personality dent or disgrace if you withdraw, then why not? In previous paragraphs, I have dwelt extensively on why you should consider not winning every argument. If you discover that the benefits of feigning ignorance are much more beneficial to effective communication and influencing, it's best that you withdraw.

Where the argument does not go to the core of your values

These are quite similar to bystander opinions. Only that bystander debates have a single intention of frustrating you. If the argument does not significantly affect your stance on any pivotal issue, you may consider letting your opponent walk away with the false win.

Concede a little to appear human

My general rule for conceding is the 9-1 principle. For every 9 arguments that you win, you are free to concede on the 10th. The idea behind this principle is to appear human to the people you aim to be an influence on.

At other times, you won't concede, but you'll genuinely make mistakes. As much as it is the human instincts to do some damage control and cover up black spots, it's honorable and human to concede. You do not want to set too lofty standards for yourself that you cannot meet. Moreover, you won't enjoy the humiliation that comes with having your cover blown.

It was Josh Billings who said, *"The man who never makes any blunders seldom makes any good hits."* This quote simply implies that you will make mistakes, and they will be a testament to more awesome strides that you will take in the future.

So, strive for perfection, but when you miss the mark, when you stutter or make that human mistake, do not feel down; neither should you feel the urge to cover it up. No follower wants a leader they cannot relate with. How you deal with your failures is a model for millions that follow in your footsteps.

Chapter 11
Influencing Technique 9 – Develop Trust and Commitment

> *A man trusts another man when*
> *he sees enough of himself in him*
> *~ Gregory David Roberts*

In law, certain relationships are categorized as fiduciary relationships. Everywhere in the world where fiduciary relationships are recognized by law, this level of human interaction is usually centered on the pillars of trust and confidence. So, an individual who is influenced by someone in a higher authority places confidence in this higher authority to always act for their benefit. A good example of a fiduciary relationship is what obtains between religious leaders and their followers. 90% of religious adherents place utmost reliance on their leaders and constantly look to them for instruction. In such instances, the religious leaders are nothing more than influencers. And if you look closely, you'll discover that their authority as influencers is built on trust.

It works the same way if you aim to influence and communicate effectively in any other way. Trust is an integral element of an influencer's career. People must be willing and able to take all your word for it. Any influence that falls short of trust will die off before you can say, Jack Robinson.

Trust is essential in your relationship with followers and in your desire to communicate effectively to people. One of the first benefits it accords you is that it ensures your security as an influencer. If people follow your lead with occasional doubts in their hearts, you can be certain that their interest in whatever value you think you put out will wear off gradually. Trust is what sustains every relationship.

You don't want to communicate with your audience being skeptical about the information they receive from you. You need the credibility to cement your status as an influencer. Otherwise, your fall to the status of a common man will be colossal.

Security aside, trust also allows positive vulnerability. Throughout the course of this book, you've learnt that influencing and communicating effectively requires you to read minds and put yourself in other people's shoes. However, without trust, you'll merely be setting yourself between a rock and a hard place. By that, I mean it will be both hard to read the minds of your audience, and still, it will be almost impossible to communicate effectively with them.

But with trust, you can engage your audience and have them open their innermost thoughts and desires to you in a flash. That's what positive vulnerability is all about. You know what the response of your audience will be to you due to trust, and you can further sell your opinions and ideas to them easily.

Mind you, trust builds more trust. If you must make mistakes, please keep it at grammatical blunders or wrong statements of opinion. Do not ever make a mistake that leaves your audience or followers in doubt of your integrity. Trust is like a pack of domino tiles. You push one tile off, and the rest fall in quick succession. So, you put the trust of your audience on red alert once, and you are bound to have a siren giving you sleepless nights till you finally fall off the cliff.

The reason why you've had to always explain and have your words subjected to a debate is because of the paucity of trust your audience placed in you. If I told you that this book was written at a secluded co-working space in Chinatown, your first instinct would be to believe me because you consider that the author of the book will surely have accurate information about where his book was written. But if someone who is closely related to me comes to give a piece of contrary information, you'll most likely debate with the person because they don't yield sufficient authority to give such a piece of information. So, you see, your endless struggles at convincing people stem from a place of lack of trust and authority.

Recognize yourself as an infallible authority and stay true

Nothing gets better than knowing how to build and develop trust. Believe me when I say that building trust is perhaps one of the toughest tasks an influencer can encounter. However, with the right techniques and tips, the stress load drops by 70%.

Here are some critical points you need to know about building trust and commitment among the people you influence.

Trust is gradual

Unlike other virtues, even if you possess 1000% integrity, it will take time for people to see it. Trust is dependent on tests. To build trust, you will have to be patient with others and remain consistent with the right mindset.

Promote joint interests

As much as you want to be famous as an influencer, your ride to fame requires wisdom and tact. Blowing your trumpet all the time will only promote a bad image of you as an influencer. Instead, seek to promote others as often as you do so to yourself. Remember, after all, that one good turn always deserves another. When you set other people up for greatness, you make them believe in your altruism on the one hand, and you tactically impose an obligation for them to do the same to you. That is the way human nature works.

Always tell the truth

When factual circumstances arise, be ready to tell the whole truth. Make it a consistent habit to be honest and plain in all your dealings with people, whether they be your superior or inferior. Telling the truth is the foundation on which everyone builds trust. You must also be prepared to tell the truth when it hurts and say "no" when it is necessary. Trying to please everyone by saying "yes" even when it is uncomfortable is dishonesty, and most people can smell that from a yard away. You'll only injure your chances at building trust.

Do not say one thing and do the other

Character dissonance is a cog in the wheel of your rise to the status of an influencer. In fact, it goes to the core of effective communication. Every human love to look beyond words and see how much actions support the words. So, you must be true to the words you say and back them up with the corresponding action.

The opening quote to this chapter is the most suitable way to end the penultimate technique to influencing and effective communication. Humans are hardwired to seek models out of people who share a striking similarity to their personality or the personality they aspire to become. Choose the latter. You tend to communicate better from a place of superiority rather than a place of equality. And the best way to approach a level of superiority without being condescending is to possess virtues that your followers admire. That chief virtue is trust. It helps you grow in other virtues. Trust helps you communicate with more confidence because you are certain that your recipients are on your side.

Trust also takes you on the wheel of fame. When you're trustworthy, people admire you and pass up your name to anyone who cares to listen. You would fare better as a local influencer with integrity than as an international star with no iota of trust. Choose what side of the divide you would rather roll with.

Chapter 12
Influencing Technique 10 – Starve Distractions, Feed Appropriate Body Language

When articulation is impossible,
gesticulation comes to the rescue
~ William Safire

The final technique to being a top influencer and an excellent communicator is to master the effective use of body language.

Body language is a mind tool. It works like the antics of a snake charmer. If actions speak louder than words, then body language convinces better than both actions and words.

Compared to other techniques you've been introduced to in this book, body language is the most practical approach to becoming a great influencer. There is no doubt that body language is most appropriate to public speaking and negotiations. But to think that those aspects are all that there is to body language is to adopt a myopic stance.

Body language cuts across every aspect of human communication. And if you are not such an individual who attempts to influence through public speaking, the benefits of body language are still an important factor you'll like to consider. So, don't flip past this chapter!

What exactly is body language?

Body language is an extremely broad term that describes the indirect communication of our feelings through several forms of body movement. Take, for example, you've been glued to a chair for hours soaking up the value in this book, and you already are developing butt pain. You may not expressly say it out loud that your butt hurts, but you'd try to adjust and conform to a new posture. That movement alone says all there is to know about your comfort.

In the same way, you can tell that an audience is bored when they begin to yawn incessantly. A passionate wink from a young man can signify a love interest or that he has an object in his eye causing discomfort. You can tell a fake smile from the squinting of the eyes and the absurd pursing of the lips. There are countless signs that you can interpret from multiple body languages.

In any communication that involves words, body language is more important than all the spoken effects combined. That's why it's easy to get lost reading books, texts, or emails. It is difficult to read body language in those instances, so you're left with the possibility of making a wrong interpretation.

Effective Communication

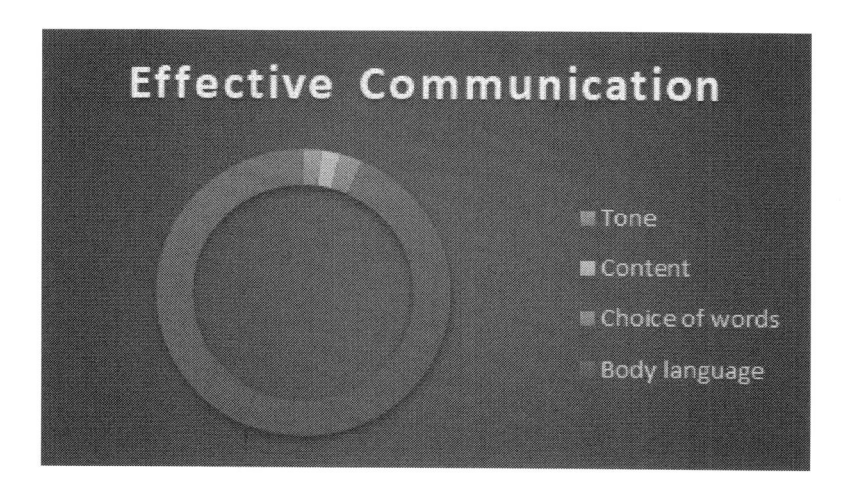

- Tone
- Content
- Choice of words
- Body language

How does body language help you as an influencer?

As an influencer looking to effectively communicate your ideas to people, body language achieves a dual benefit. First, it helps you attract your audience to your communication style, and on the flip side, it helps you read the room – your audience's response to you.

While we've dealt extensively with understanding your audience and reading their minds, this chapter aims to give a comprehensive guide to attract your audience through body language. So, you will find little advice on how to read body language here (chapters 4 & 5 already did justice to that). But for the most part, you'll find out how to "SPEAK" body language.

Signs of a Disengaged Audience

A disengaged audience is an audience that is out of your psychological control. You can neither influence nor communicate effectively to this audience type. You can tell a disengaged audience through the following body language forms:

- Very minimal facial connection or eye-to-eye contact with you. A disengaged audience will usually consist of people looking into an empty space or fixing their gaze on objects around them rather than at you.

- The body is turned away from you. They have their bodies postured in a way that signifies disinterest. Their heads may be downcast, and their bodies sitting slumped.

- Distracted activity. Disengaged audiences are either scribbling or keeping themselves busy by fiddling with their phones or picking clothes.

Look, Touch, and Move like a God

Knowing the signs of a disengaged audience is more of a problem if you don't know how to buy them back. Your best bet is to use a body language strategy that they love and understand. In short, you must look, touch, and move like a god.

Keep a perfect posture

Whether it's a casual gathering or a formal occasion, your posture says a lot about you. You must therefore endeavor to keep a perfect posture both while standing and while sitting. As a rule, do not slouch. Keep your head up. Stand or sit upright and keep your hands right by your sides. Folding your arms akimbo or placing them on your hips could pass the wrong message.

Keep your hands off your face

You tend to let off an aura of timidity and dishonesty when you fiddle with parts of your face.

Keep your hands firmly in place where others can see them.

Gesticulate often

Gesticulations give more life to communication than most people can imagine. Gesticulating with your hands usually lets off a feeling that you're willing to share ideas. Spread your hands apart, make numerical signs with your fingers where appropriate, raise your hands and create signs corresponding to what you intend to say. As much as you do this, keep your arms close to your body; otherwise, you will risk overexpression – people may focus on your gestures more than your ideas.

Smile and keep your head up

Your smile is the doorway to positivity. So, smile as often as possible. You must also ensure that you look upright and refrain from leaning to either side.

Steer clear of distractions

Distractions are a primary enemy of the exercise of influence. When amidst people as an influencer, you must ensure to actively keep your concentration on the people you aim to communicate with. That is because people tend to pay you back in your own coin. If you seem distracted in your communications with them, they will most likely take you for a ride when it's time to exert your influence. And by then, damage control will be mostly impossible.

As with almost every technique in this book, practice makes perfect. Keep on communicating with body language in little quantities, and in no time, you will be dexterous at it.

Chapter 13
Plan a Thousand Times over

Give me six hours to chop down a tree,
and I will spend the first four sharpening the ax.
~ Abraham Lincoln

You have gotten this far in what is meant to be a step-by-step guide to influencing through effective communication. If there is one lesson you must hold on to, it must be that there's a long walk to the lofty status of an influencer. Moreover, effective communication abilities won't grow on you overnight. It's a fairly long and intensive process. And as such, you must devote time, intellect, and physical strength to seeing your dreams work out.

All these techniques to being a respectable influencer underscore the importance of planning.

Planning is the art of seeing a goal far off and preparing for its actualization long before.

Be it a short-term engagement to speak to people or communicate through entertainment forms, it requires intense planning. You must start working towards your final goal as though it is to be achieved tomorrow.

The story of an individual who aims to be an influence in the long term is not any different. It's a career path that can shape your life's trajectory. I bet you it's not an event you would want to stumble upon without adequate preparation. To be sure, effective communication and influencing demands mental, emotional, financial, and relational planning.

Before I go on to give you deep insights into these forms of planning, the story of how Israel planned one of the most surprising conquests in modern history is instructive here.

History tells us that Israel had always been a nation-state existing since the 9th Century BCE. However, in AD 70, the ancient Israeli state will fade into thin air under the expansive Roman Empire. While the big re-emergence of this nation is traced to the 1948 Arab-Israeli, the nation cemented its power status with the famous Six-Day War of 1967. The history of the Six-Day War will go down as one of the most strategic wars in the annals of history.

In 1967, Israel began an assault on the biggest Arab nations: Egypt, Jordan, Syria, and Iraq. The Israeli troops were grossly outnumbered, having just over 250,000 troops and deploying 50,000. On the other divide, the Arab states had over 540,000 troops and deployed about 240,000. The Israeli weaponry was also a mere pinch of salt compared to what the Arab nations had in their arsenal.

Yet, six days after the war began, it was already ended – in favor of the underdog, Israel. While sharing the reasons for the success, an Israeli military commander named Mordecai Hod stated that *"for sixteen years, we had been planning what took place in those first 80 minutes. We lived with that plan, we ate with it, we slept with it. We never stopped improving it."*

That statement should provide the motivation you need on the importance of planning. Who would have thought that a war would have been in the works for 16 years? While this book does not sanction war or violence, it nonetheless gives you every go-ahead to plan. After all, if you don't learn from history, you're bound to repeat its mistakes.

The journey to influence requires planning and a striving towards perfection, and only those who devote the resources it requires will make the final cut.

So, what should your planning span across?

- Mental planning: Here is where you decide how you want to be an influence. If you desire to be a public speaker, a leader or a politician, here's the stage where you take up a course, go for public speaking training, attend debates, and make yourself visible at events.

- Emotional planning: You must prepare for the days where you'll be jeered, pushed to the wall while maintaining your convictions. There are days where you'll be faced with threats for your truths, but you must never be deterred.

- Financial planning: As an influencer and effective communicator, you'll need the platforms to amplify your voice. And you must know that they come at financial costs. Save up or invest, so you won't be caught off guard when the need to spend arises.

- Relational planning: At this level of planning, your main aim is to build quality and mutually beneficial relationships. Surround yourself with loyal people who will open opportunities for you and for whom you will do the same.

Effective Communication as a Battle of Ideologies

As an influencer, you're bound to communicate with people. What I've come to discover is that at every stage, there's an ideology that goes against yours. In the end, the individual who can effectively communicate his opinions, beliefs, and narratives will be the one fit enough to be considered an influence.

That's why you must never take your task with levity. Be knowledgeable about what you represent and be confident in your abilities.

Plan the How and What beforehand

At every stage of your influence, there is a "what" and a "how" to discover. Well, for the records, the "who" and "where" questions are settled to a great extent. It's YOU against the WORLD.

The "what" on your road to effective communication and influencing is the area of influence you intend to follow. You must go on a discovery of what treasure you aim to pass on to the world at large. It may be influencing and communicating to people through comedy, sports, music, politics, medicine, law, science, business, or engineering. The "what" is your niche. And like every other part of influencing, you don't stumble upon it. You must prepare ahead. Study wide about your niche, have mentors in your field and develop your knowledge base.

The "how" on the path to influence is your channel of communication. Remember that influencing is akin to you being able to communicate effectively to people, leave them in awe, and draw them to yourself as followers. So, pick a medium of expression that you are most comfortable with and plan. While many "whats" necessarily come with their "how," others may not. The onus is on you to figure it out and plan towards being the greatest in your medium!

The world is plagued by mediocrity, and there is a choice the future generation beckons on you to make. Will you leave a mark of influence and communicate your ideas like one of the wisest humans to set foot on the planet? Or will you sit in dysfunction and pass on your duty?

Your answer ends this book.

Disclaimer

This book contains opinions and ideas of the author and is meant to teach the reader informative and helpful knowledge while due care should be taken by the user in the application of the information provided. The instructions and strategies are possibly not right for every reader and there is no guarantee that they work for everyone. Using this book and implementing the information/recipes therein contained is explicitly your own responsibility and risk. This work with all its contents, does not guarantee correctness, completion, quality or correctness of the provided information. Misinformation or misprints cannot be completely eliminated.

Printed in Great Britain
by Amazon